with wide open eyes

edited & compiled by

Deepali Shriram Giri

Inkfeathers Publishing

With Wide Open Eyes
Edited & Compiled by Deepali Shriram Giri
Print Edition

First Published in India in 2021
Inkfeathers Publishing
New Delhi 110095

www.inkfeathers.com

co-authored by

Paola Mora ~ Luna Adair ~ A'Danya Blake ~ Midhun BM ~ Jarod Wabick ~ Liz Amsel ~ Uthra Baskaran ~ Ann Chaiti Sarkar ~ Sukti Sisodiya ~ Annapurani Vaidyanathan ~ Earljanne Ofalla ~ Isheta Boruah ~ Sarvani Sita ~ Preeti Kale ~ Inkforyou ~ Akshay Rathore ~ Yukti Arya ~ Shikha Sengar ~ Juwairiyah Tariq Sayeed ~ Abby Kayy ~ Najam Us Saher ~ Abhishek Kulkarni ~ Madhurya Kommuri ~ Dazima Rai ~ Sushma Chaudhary ~ Alka Prakash ~ Tugce Gokoglu ~ Shivani Kaushik ~ Tejasvee Nagar ~ Snehal Agarwal ~ Irenaa Malik ~ Rahul Nayak ~ Padmini Peteri ~ Saloni Wagle ~ Prerna Agrawal ~ Shreya Khemani ~ Uzlifat Zahoor ~ Namita Das ~ Mohammed Mudassir ~ Neha Prashar ~ Meenakshi Ramswamy ~ Vaishnavi Singh ~ Shikha Sharda ~ Divya Bora ~ The Wanderer Mind ~ Nirosha Tomy ~ Deepesha J. ~ Jagruthi Kommuri ~ Disha Shinde ~ Swetha Nair

contents

meet the compiler

Deepali Shriram Giri

Deepali is a writer, poet, and dental aspirant who's currently pursuing her bachelor's degree in Dental Surgery from Nair Hospital Dental College, Mumbai. Poetry is in her blood as her father Shriram Giri is a well-known Marathi Gazalkar and Poet. Her house feels more like a library than home.

Her writing style is influenced by rebellious and real poetry. She prefers talkative, powerful, and realistic poetry which would strike the heart of the reader. Society and human minds are inspirations of her writing. Her Instagram handle @silent_rebel20 has been created with the same inspiration. She strongly believes that no matter in which genre the authors write, their literary expressions should not be limited to a specific society, country, or group, rather should have a comradeship of universal consciousness.

English writers like George Eliot, Virginia Woolf and O. Henry have a significant influence on her writing. She loves to read poems of Indian poet and lyricist "Sahir Ludhianvi" and Punjabi poet "Pash".

She is also an art enthusiast and interested in studying the history of art. The life and works of impressionist artist Vincent van Gogh and Fauvism artist Henri Matisse inspire her. She likes to visit beaches with friends on weekends and loves to read books and play harmonium in her free time.

compiler's note

Working on the anthology "With Wide Open Eyes" was an exciting journey. Connecting with new writers from all over the world, grasping their writing cultures, their styles of expression and understanding a "poet" inside them was a real pleasure for me. It was something different than my regular poetry and blog writing. I got a chance to learn new skills and to explore and develop my working style. Inkfeathers Team was there with me throughout this entire process of collecting poems and compiling them into a book. The guidance provided by such an experienced team made it much easier to create this book.

It's hard to express emotions and formless thoughts which seem complicated and baseless from outside. But these poets of talent have done a magnificent job in bringing these emotions to life through their verses.

When these hidden emotions scream to make themselves heard, and when these screams are silenced by the world, these poets seek comfort in the poetic art of writing.

In these lines from the poem, "Drowning, Again" the poet has expressed her vulnerability indicatively.

"Drop by drop, my lungs fill
Shouting is never an option
I was meant to feel this."

In another poem, "I Killed My Love" the poet reveals the toxic dominance of our society over an individual person.

"It's a power held by those hands not mine
It is either this or that, like nickel and dime".

The poems in this anthology have the power to shake your mind. They can break you into pieces and then mould you again with a completely new "mind-set". You will be able to observe different shades of the human mind while reading poems from different cultures and styles all over the world.

With Wide Open Eyes is a conscious look on the path of life and society by the poets.

with wide
open eyes

glad you left

And in the mirror
I could see
The strength,
The love,
The grace,
The happiness
And the joy
You left me
When you walked away;
And also
The pain
And the tears
I dropped
When you stayed.

-Paola Mora

love chaos

I lost you in the dark space
In my mind created due to
insecurities and trust issues,
I lost you in a place where
I can't find you no matter how
Hard I try, I can't see you
In this dark space which is
Consuming me inside,
It's getting hard to breathe
You are my only hope of
Getting out of here but
I have lost you in this dark.

-Luna Adair

on carefully curated pyromania

Ashes follow me everywhere,
As if I were their sworn guide and they got lost;
The smell of singed hope and charged anger
Billow like flying kites in the air
Crowning me.

I think I have my own little hell division
Crackling in my hollowed
Footsteps, teeming like pressure in a lidded
Pot under the folds of my clothes
Like a storm in a tiny bottle
Ready to explode.
Tell them that when they look in all the places
Where they want me to be:
As sure as I wail in want to be free,
They will never find me.

-A'Danya Blake

perturbation

Things went okay,
Like any other day.
But deep inside I fear,
Of the pain I'd have to bear.
When you are gone,
And I am left alone.

How long should I hide?
Behind the veil of my pride,
Denying the turning tide.
Within which I am caught,
Without a way out.

As the Doom draws close,
Left with no plans to propose.
To resist the Grim Reaper,
Hungry for your soul.

I loath to confront,
What is in front.
Stuck in a stalemate,
With the irrefutable fate.

-Midhun B M

lonely crow

Jazz came slow
Out the radio
Took its time

Like the sun did
Coming up
This morning

Though I'm still
Not quite sure
That it did.

In fact it seemed
The only things
Movin' fast
This morning
Were my thoughts &
This lonely crow
Cuttin' through the sky.

-Jarod Wabick

there is a piece of you

There is a piece of you
Left behind in me
Like a forgotten t-shirt,
Tucked away
Inside the crooks of my soul
To be found at a later date
When I'll once again
Feel my heart
Shatter like glass
On a hardwood floor
As I carefully
Pick up the pieces;
Terrified to cut the tips of my fingers
And bleed out
What little is left of you
In my veins.

-Liz Amsel

drowning, again

Engulfed in the dark,
I refuse to switch on the light
I can see it, it's so very close.
But I've been avoiding the pain,
It's been suppressed for too long
And like scars, pain doesn't fade either.

Gently, the pain takes over,
Overwhelming my senses
Showing me the way,
Pitching me in black.

This is where I am meant to be, it says,
an ocean drowns me.

Drop by drop, my lungs fill.
Shouting is never an option,
I was meant to feel this
I give myself up, thought by thought
Feeling the water seep in through my skin
I become blue, a beautiful colour,
The colour of sadness, and of beauty.

It has been done; I'm drowned.
But I know I'll have to swim back up.

This is a sea of my own doing
And death is nowhere close.

I clamber for the weapon, the antidote.
My head pounding with adrenaline
Flight or fight, I cannot tell,
But I know this is the way out.

I grasp it tightly, feeling power
A control that I had forfeited.
Clean and deep, I feel a new burn
And slowly, the drops come
Blood red and rushing free.
I release my ocean,
Bidding it farewell until next time.

-Uthra Baskaran

if a serpent had fingers

During nightfall they change,
Deceitful eyes collapse to sliver.
I shiver,
Shake myself awake
To the rubble of their masterpiece,
Manifested in the wake
Of the moonlight.
Voices start to layer in the distance
Coming to congregate,
Now we just wait in the pale of the moonlight.
Purgatory is nice
The trickles now arrive,
For destruction's what they strive for
Trace my silhouette in dew drops
Trickles down stream that runs down the rocks
If a serpent had fingers
Then this would linger
Through the presence of the sun.
Then there'd be none.
Then there'd be none.

-*Ann Chaiti Sarkar*

ephemeral

We buzz around
And the energy I get from falling into
You
Starts to make something.
Like pollination.
So close to giving life.

And then it dies,
Because my feelings have a shorter lifespan
Than male bees.

I can be sweet like the richest honey, but I still sting
So
You either lick your lips
Or gnash your teeth.

-A'Danya Blake

forever yearning

Ignore me. It's fun.
Laugh at me. It's fun, really
Dismiss me. No, really, it's fun.

Hiding behind this pretty façade
Indifferent, perfect, healing.
I can't explain myself either way
How can I say that I am crying
Shaking like a child, just because
My friend hasn't spoken all day.
How do I explain to them
That an idiot stole my heart
Which I am yet to steal back.
I call it all fun and games,
I laugh at your pettiness
And shoulder your rants, hoping
That maybe you'll do the same,
For me, someday. Yes, it's true
I'm selfish, more than you.
This is a war zone, of feelings,
Emotions that will pepper you
With bullets until you're ripped apart,
No longer recognizable.
A shadow of days past.

When I tell you something and
You turn away, laughing it off,

I laugh too, and crack a smile
For that's what it is, and
I do not know why
I keep expecting anything otherwise.

-Uthra Baskaran

what numbness looks like

I can't breathe,
And yet, there's enough air
In my heart
To revive a thousand dying mortals.

I feel as cold as the heart
Of the one who caused this.
And yet, there's enough fire
To burn down entire cities.

That's the thing about feeling nothing.
You can't decipher yourself
For there is nothing to decipher,
There is just plain, agonising silence
And a painful void,
You're drowning inside your own self,
And there's nothing you can do about it
—feeling silence.

-Sukti Sisodiya

the tells

When I am sad,
I sop, and smell like wet paper.
When I am angry,
I smoulder, and smell like burnt paper.
Most times,
I smell like wet, burnt paper.
How brilliant it is
With a love like ink-stained palms
That clench like a Venus flytrap when emotions land in that
pit of blazing frustration.
On a good, bad day
There'll be differently coloured ink stains to flaunt.
I know how to char everything except my unbecoming habits.
I just know how to wipe the testimonial soot of those off my
scarred
Fingertips
I just know how to peel the potent pieces of potential poems
off of my troubled skin
And crumbling paper
In small bits.
I just know how to flush all the betraying tears back and pray
The smile pretending perfect sanity still fits,
Never publicly slips.

-*A'Danya Blake*

testing the waters

My feet are stuck
With indecision.

Running away
Isn't a habit
They've been taught –
Oh, they're quite used
To being run over
When they're no longer needed,
To being grounded
When fear cripples them
To the last farthing,
To being judged
Beyond reason,
To being subjected
To constant supervision.
But they're now
Caught in a quicksand
Of choices
They can't choose between –
Staying back,
Listening to voices
They don't trust
And letting a marionettist
Pull the strings
Or
Flying away
To a new, unfamiliar world
That would force them
To chop off their wings.

Why can toes not
Test the waters
Of the unfamiliar paths
They want to tread upon,
And then just
Lie back
To simply watch the
Journey unfold?

-Annapurani Vaidyanathan

the sculptor

I'm sorry if I have to remold you one more time,
Your inability to move makes this look like a crime.
I know you'll stay quiet but would still try to refuse,
But the imperfections in your mold have got me seduced.

The length of your limbs would need readjustments
Please understand that you only deserve compliments.
The shape of your torso can easily be refined,
All I want is for you to be well designed.

I feel your neck with my hands as it makes an impression,
My nails dig deep and cut with a jagged incision.
I tug and pull your head away from your body
Your impression less face seems to show melancholy.

What I'm doing is not a sign of dissatisfaction,
Remolding you to be flawless is my form of affection.
I kiss your forehead then begin to dismember you
Arm by arm, leg by leg, you watch as I do.

Believe me when I say that this is unavoidable,
I can hear you detest through your weak mumble.
I came close to your ear to deliver a soft whisper,
I told you to be quiet and to stop your useless whimper,

You might question my love, but believe me it's true
For me to show hate, give pain, or hurt you,
I have to forget and leave you at the back of my mind

I'll do what I think is best until all is well aligned.

-Earljanne Ofalla

blurred reminiscence

O dear,
What have we become?
I still let my senses reminisce about your skin's smell, little
sweet and bits of mint.
Do you still remember mine? You used to say it reminds you
of the season autumn; beauty and crisps.
But doesn't everything perish in autumn?

What have we become?
I let my eyes lose in deep thoughts of you, ruffled, side swept
hair, smirk-smiles and Mongolian eyes.
Do you still let lose yours too?
You used to say, "Burgundy waves of the sea as such your hair,
which pours down my face."
Do her waves act in that way too?

What have we become?
I let my ears get lose amidst the memoirs of your heavy voice,
witty remarks, and coltish chuckle.
But I am sure, well maybe, that it's 'she' who is the harbinger
of your euphoria now.

Well,
I guess, now it's just that; what have I become?
It's queer, I only have the aid of the memories of my senses
to resurrect you from the abandoned land,
I do not know how long

those memories will keep you awaken in me before it succumbs in itself to nothingness.

Yours
~~Not anymore~~

-Isheta Boruah

beautiful destiny

Falling in the pit
Of your love was
Never a choice it
Was a beautiful
Destiny which was
Meant to happen,
Every moment
Spent with you feels
As if sprinkled with
Magical stardust.

-Luna Adair

tears

Tears,
The inevitable grief
That sweeps down,
Cremating every cell that comes down
Sucking calm and relief.

Tears,
The fragments of memories
Our brain will never forget
Our heart will never forgive.
The reminder of our realities.

Tears,
The sign of our resilience
When adversities take over,
The hearse to carry cadaver
Of our rotting soul.
The symbol of our
Dwindling patience.

Tears,
The expression of pain,
The world never cares about.
The drops of stormy rain
Which subside
For the dawn to break again.

-Sarvani Sita

poison

"Pick your poison," he says.
The city looks drunk, with blotches of streetlights here and
there.
Your 3 am playlist keeps getting interrupted by sirens, catcalls,
and thoughts.
You take another drag of your cigarette and scrutinize his
movements the best you can.
An assortment of intoxicants sit cozily beside him, waiting to
be exploited.

Attempting to brand your personality through the lingering
taste of cheap booze, he patiently waits for your answer.
Perhaps he thought you were in pain, turning to the sour and
bitter jolt of vodka to numb it.
Or maybe somebody with damaged goods,
wasting away nights by the fireplace and a glass of bourbon to
warm your broken spirits.
Maybe, he thought you were too delicate and mellow to
handle those and coveted tequila instead
He puts his palm over yours, urging you to answer.
"Poetry," you mumble.
He looks baffled and opens his mouth to repeat his question.
"Poetry is my poison," you blow out the smoke and stub out
the cigarette.

"I get tipsy on words and high on emotions.
I can see eight colors in the rainbow and hear things you want
to say but never will.
I slit my own wrist with a feathered pen before starting a new
verse.

I see the sky crying for help when you see the twinkling stars.
I save my emotions on the waterline of my eyes, because the
more you show, the more they strip you down."
He waits for you to go on, but the words are resting on your
toxoid tongue.
You know he wants to comfort you and whisper sweet
nothings to calm you down.
He aches to tell you that it's all going to be alright.
"I know everything will be alright," you sigh.
"I didn't say anything," he says, looking astonished.
You let your gaze shift towards the sky and sadly smile.
"The stars are sparkling awfully bright tonight."

-Preeti Kale

black and white

25

With an exhale,
You breathed
So much color
Into my life,
And as quickly
As an inhale,
It became
Black and white.

-Inkforyou

disillusioned

Is this the end of hope?
The demise of light
Or is this
The darkest hour before the dawn?

When you feel broken
Or burnt, or frozen with fear
Do you stand and face it
Or are you more like me
And run away and try to disappear?

I can't control this anymore.
This poetry just flies
Out of my veins
And straight into the paper,
Just like my life.
One second, one minute, one decade
Out of the clock

We are alive
In our most vulnerable moments
Or are we?
Or maybe you are.

I am just more dead than ever
I wish this could stop.

It's a cycle you know?
And cycles repeat
Mistakes, pleasure
Denial, guilt
Denial, pleasure
Mistakes.

Do you find this disorderly?
Out of rhythm,
Devoid of style,
Screaming for attention?
Welcome to my world.
It sucks, you're going to love it.

-Akshay Rathore

horizon

It is good
watching people's talent, success,
Happiness, achievements.
It seems clear like a blue sky,
Sometimes cloudy,
But at the end, a beautiful blue sheet of joy.
What's hidden below
Are the failures,
Downs with little ups at points.
The missed opportunities,
Misunderstood thoughts, all in the horizon.

Horizon,
The infinite space of hard work,
Passion for achieving the level,
That can satisfy your living.
It's not just about
An Artist who creates new world onto canvas or
A Writer who decorates his thoughts on paper.
It's about everyone with their own strength of creating magic.
Take a span of time
To perceive then to pursue your potency.

-Yukti Arya

someone like you

We sat opposite each other.
My eyes staring at the table,
You staring at me.

You trying too hard to talk
And me trying too hard to listen.
The distance between us
Was just a touch away,
But we were too afar.
The voice of Adele
Singing 'Someone like you'
Filled the background.

I smiled, thinking about us.
The day you promised me
A warm heart and home.
An old memory which now
Turned into a private joke.
'Why are you smiling?' you asked.
I didn't utter a word about us.
I didn't utter a word about you.
I didn't utter a word about home.

I sat there like an old book
Which is too perishable
To go into naïve hands.

It just stays in one corner
Where all the classics are kept
And it's now too tired to pass on in different hands.
So, this book doesn't like strangers anymore.

I wonder if you still see
My face in strangers though.
If a girl removing the strands of her hair
From her face reminds you of me,
Or a distant laugh you hear in the café
Makes you look out for me.
I wonder if I still breathe somewhere
In the corners of your mind.
I hope, I still breathe.

'How are you?' you asked multiple times
And I didn't know what to say.
'Sometimes it lasts in love but
Sometimes it hurts instead.'
This is what Adele said.
And I remembered about the time
When you showed me
The picture of another girl
And how you thought she loved you
More than I ever could.

I stood up to leave.
The café was a trap.
You were a trap.

There were many things left unsaid.
An explanation for every rose
Left behind in my diary.

A story for my shattered heart
And a broken home.
But I smiled again, because I knew
That I will find someone like you again
But that someone will be nothing like you.
That someone won't be you.

-Shikha Sengar

i'll rise again, anew

Crippled for life, they made sure I was,
Clipping my wings, they sneered about,
Iron restricting my tiny claws,
They bickered and bickered, yet, pacific I was,
A cold fish, they spat on me.
O' thou, thee doused the ignited bosom,
But the Law of Nature dilapidate ne'er,
Fueling the candle that is my soul,
Brightening the well in the desert dunes,
The deeper you hit the more water it'll hold,
An oasis rekindling the travel-worn,
A city emerging from the shadow doomed.
I'll rise again with a fury, anew!

-Juwairiyah Tariq Sayeed

invincible

I feel I don't exist
As darkness subsists
The battles of my mind.
The wind doesn't
Acknowledge my presence,
Neither does the ground
Echo my strides
in the still night.
Like a ghost,
I wander with no soul.
But the moonlight
That reflects my shadow
In the darkness
Thinks otherwise.

-Abby Kayy

over the years

Unlike the happiness that compels,
My sorrows inspired me.
My grief pushed me forward
And my loneliness motivated me.

Unlike the ideal persons that aspire,
My heart had an image of a person I must not be
My memories quenched the raging fire
And my solitude kept me going.

Unlike a soul that touches many hearts,
I was alone with my broken self,
My unaccomplished dreams I desired
And my hope faltered, but never faded.

Unlike the positivity that helps,
My accusations tempted me to prove them wrong,
My guilt changed the thoughts
And my regrets reformed me.

Unlike the perfections that help
My flaws I embraced,
My restlessness gave me hope
And my imperfections just perfected me all the way.

-Najam Us Saher

mystique

I want to take you in my arms,
Hand in hand just walk with you
Breezy may be evenings,
Cold may be nights.

Together we walk miles and miles,
Together we feel content and reprise,
Words may take break,
But silence would, though, speak.

I may have a dark side, but
 You are my mystique.

-Abhishek Kulkarni

is someone there

My hands sweat,
My heart aches,
My body it shakes.
But is someone there,
Who even care?

Sometimes my eyes rain,
Succumbing to this pain.
To the demons in my mind I'm chained.
But is someone there,
Who even care?

I pull myself near,
Trembling with fear.
My silent cries which no body hear.
But is someone there,
Who even care?

What about the times, when it's
Not my eyes but my heart that bleeds,
Into depths of trauma it leads,
And I'm left quite indeed.
But is someone there,
Who even care?

My room doors I close,
Laying numb on the floor,
Crying more and more.
But is someone there,
Who even care?

This agony it kills,
I gulp many pills,
Oh God! Like hell it feels.
But is someone there,
Who even care?

There are wounds so deep,
Which I myself am afraid to peep,
And this to myself I keep.
But is someone there,
Who even care?

On papers, walls I scribble,
Wanting myself to strangle,
With pain I struggle.
Life or death-what to choose?
Fed up and my control I lose.
But is someone there,
Who even care?

My strength as a prey to the sorrow it bends,
To kill myself my heart tends.
Only if there's someone to befriend
Whose ears they could lend,
My wounds would definitely mend.
But is someone there,
Who even care?

Is someone there
Who really care??
Someone when I dial,
To stay a little while,
Walk the extra mile,
To bring back my smile?

Oh wait, let me ask
Can you be that someone?
Your smile can make someone's day brighter,
The time you spend can make their heart lighter.
Love, care, kindness— they have a great power,
Underestimate it never,
Trust me you can change lives forever.
So why not?
Let's shout out.

Hey, beautiful soul,
I know, in your heart, there's a hole.
But let's not make it a big deal,
I promise to help you heal.
It's not a big matter,
Things will eventually get better.
Forget your fears,
I'll be there to wipe your tears.
It's alright,
Don't give in to your plight,
You can defeat the devils in your fight,
Because you, my dear
Are a warrior with might!
And some day to the world proudly
You'd say "I am victorious" loudly!

-Madhurya Kommuri

eros of night

Embracing the blanket of night,
Eyeing at city covered in moonlight.
Nights are beautiful and divine,
It's the peace we all seek to recline.

No one dares to know the struggles
That burn inside ones' heart
When the world goes into a deep silent,
There emerges agony loud and violent.

Drowning in our self-accusations,
Struggling with terrifying emotions.
Some dance with sync in rhythm
Some feel the tenderness in silence

The night is calm with dense emotions,
Knowing how intense it gets
Knowing the love it can reflect
This is the night we all embrace.

-Dajeema Rai

we are nothing but

We are nothing but, stars
That once shined,
We are nothing but, flowers
That once bloomed.

We are nothing but, lovebirds
That once cared,
We are nothing but, strangers
That once loved.

-Sushma Chaudhary

neither weak nor strong

Slamming the door,
Foot hard on the floor,
Tears brimming the eyes,
The screaming voice freezing to ice.

Oh, so I ran straight to my room,
A thing I had never realized before,
But the four-wall surrounded space,
Was another place; it made me doom.

Hours have passed,
No movement in me,
Am I dead?
Arose the question within.

Soon, the lashes danced,
The music being the alarm clock,
Eyes still baggy, with a few drops,
And a visible trail, which dried below the spot.

Where am I now?
The place is the same.
But the vibe here,
Is something I have felt again and again.

My feet set ahead,
Crossing the gates, I reach my classroom.
There's none, yes I reached first,
Just like any other day, so I could at least assure myself a seat.

The window, the same window,
I guess it must remember the taste of my blood,
My head slammed against it,
More than any cleaning agent.

My gaze is fixed, as usual,
On the desk,
Fearing to be lifted,
To meet the eyes, of any of the assaulters.

They entered, one after the other,
Tears pooled my eyes, fearing the figures,
My heart shifted to my throat,
My tongue bleeding between my teeth.

It was when I felt the floor,
My hairs sprawled over my visage,
I felt the hard cold floor,
Even it denied me with its cold.

"Get up you bitch", I heard the cry,
Fearing the assault, I tried,
But a scream left my throat,
As I felt my twisting foot.

I tried to get up again,
But all in vain,
All I wanted, was to run away,
To the place where I could feel some sun.

I heard the bell, and the teacher entered,
He spared me a glance, and everyone returned,
I sat at my seat, all the while,
Receiving the pellets, waiting for my demise.

The bell rang again, I left the room,
I stood behind the door huge,
Pulling up my sleeves,
Revealing the marks, I have been hiding all along.

There's a bruise at my elbow,
A burn mark near my neck,
White bandages covering my stomach,
And a stitch enhancing my brows.

I stood up, to get out,
It was when, I felt a sting in my foot,
Focusing my eyes to the spot,
I saw red liquid, bathing my socks.

"He's the minister's kid, sorry we can't help"
The words echoed in my ears,
What could I have said,
I am a kid to none at all.

The bulling continued,
Like any other day,
Food being thrown at me,
The ketchup painting my white shirt.

The pen being pierced,
Deep into my skin,
Adding another hole,
To the already existing ones.

That was the day it happened,
That was the place which sensed it all,
My doom, my demise, my suicide,
Or my relief you may call.

Pulling out the shining thin slit out of my pocket,
It was going to be the end of my disgrace,
Clutching it between my fingers,
My eyes, full of tears.

I brought my fist up to my face,
On the blue vein, it was placed,
Inhaling deep, the last time my lungs could,
The thin metal did it's work.

The world seemed to spin around,
My head getting heavy,
I could hear the liquid dripping on the ground,
Closing my eyes shut was all I could do.

For the first time,
I didn't feel the floor cold
Maybe now was the time,
It finally accepted me.

The last thoughts that came into my mind,
I was not born weak,
I was not born strong,
It was this world which determined me,
As I am now.
I tried my best,
To be strong.
But my fate had plans,
I was accepted by none, while alive,

Maybe through this path,
I may be called as the one I am,
And not just the one bullied by all.

I was not born weak or strong,
It was the society that determined me as the one I am
I was just a child, alone
Alone was, I guess, my fault.

-Alka Prakash

now that i have loved you

Now that I have loved you,
There is no turning back.
My eyes have seen your eyes,
My hands have held your hands.
Bring me far away
Where no one can find us,
A new beginning,
The mountains will hide us.
Be my sun and I will be your moon.
Be the days to my nights
Not only to live with you,
But also to die with you.

-Tugce Gokoglu

it is for you to know

"Is it the end? Or the beginning?
Or is it too insignificant to exist?"
I asked the sea at the seashore.
It roared, "It's for you to know!
For I may tell the folklore,
But then, it is for you to know!"

I let my skin feel the sand underneath
Mighty water touching my feet
As if saying humbly,
"I bow to you and you bow to me,
Acknowledging the me in you and the you in me."
I asked the water, "what if I want to be
As calm and ferocious as thee?"
It said, "You are what you want to be,
But it's not for me to guide the fleet."

Another day and the wild wind blew.
Birds sang, the wind whistled,
And the leaves danced on the snow.
"O Wind! O Wind! How can I smile
When I feel so low?
My heart is broken, and the love is gone."
The wind rattled at the windowsill,
"No matter who comes and who goes,
Believe in thee and rise when you are low.
For that is the way of life, it will always flow.
But it is for you to find it slow."

Cold winters came and came with it
The urge to sit near the fiery wood pit.
The sparks rose in the fireplace.
I could feel the warmth as the fire was lit.
It's when I asked,
"I am wise and old now, you know,
Still will you guide me to the path to the heavenly hill?"
The blazing fire replied in a split,
"I can light the path, the path to all the hills,
Or can burn the world
With the demons in it.
You can do it too, but who am I to say?
All you have to find is the power of will."

Seasons passed and the years yawned,
Another day came and a new boy in the sun shone.
Wind played with his hair
And the water flowed to and fro.

At the seashore, he asked for help
To find all that he had lost.
And the sea said, "I know the quest you are on,
But destination, it is for you to know!"

-Shivani Kaushik

stayed for long

I loved to stay at the park for long,
For the fountains cherished crystal clear moonlight.
If there would have been a clearer reflection, within the waters.
It was out of sight.
Monsoons were damp and roads were probably hollow mud
filled islands.
The poet in me usually got attracted to the scenario!
This time, it was sweeping away the park's sand.
There were chances to develop a temperature,
The pressure of releasing the tears while not being noticed,
Greater was it!
"All I wanted was rain to cry."
Compliments and a helping hand, as if the sky,
Had hugged my soul!
Yesterday, he took me out for coffee.
Yesterday, my journal noted down the smiles and he asked me
to picture a doodle of him!
Today, he changed the scenario.
Today, he scribbled my face with a black marker and put a
layer of names.
Seems like the 11:11 wishes don't always work.
I stayed at the park today, a little more than yesterday!
And tomorrow a better half of me fell in love with my
existence!
Yesterday, my voice was his voice!
Today, my voice is my voice!

Some days I still slide back to the park,
When the puddle of emotions overcome the existential

pressure!
Then, I come back and stay.

Stay with my journal which has a part consumed for me and
nature.
You would entangle my mind, but not my soul,
Flowers and rains have looked up for me, more than you ever
did.

-Tejasvee Nagar

abandoned

The bed creaked every time I moved, as it was unstable;
And it was the closest that I had to a cradle.
The fan whizzed all night, and it was the only lullaby,
The chipped off paint on the walls made me want to say the place good-bye.

Even the smell of half cooked food made my underfed tummy rumble,
Standing in queue to use the loo, I always mumbled,
"What did I ever do wrong?"
"Why did my parents leave me in an orphanage?"

-Snehal Agarwal

prayer of love

On some days, I wish I could curl up inside the blanket with
you,
And our intertwined fingers would dance together on the
rhythm of our heart beats,
On other days, I just wish to hear your voice a little longer
than just 3.5 minutes,
And I almost stop myself from telling you to stay a little
longer,
And in exchange of that, I just hold myself tight and close my
eyes and tell you to come back soon.
On some days, I am a complete mess, and my voice shakes as I
speak,
And you ask me if everything's fine and even before I answer it,
you, love, know it all
and gather my pieces and put them together so beautifully,
On other days, you bring all the butterflies in the world alive,
You put a smile on my face so wide,
That even after the call's disconnected all I can do is smile with
tears running down my eyes,
On some days, I wake up to your voice,
Your voice, my love, plays like a favourite song on repeat.
On other days, I am so restless to hear your voice for even a
second that it plays like a prayer in my head,
Until you call back again.
On some days, you're my favourite playlist,
On others, a prayer,
A prayer to find an escape from the reality.
A prayer crying out to be in your arms one last time,
Before you leave.
On some days, I write you pages and pages of poetry

Spilling out love
In the language that we best know.

On other days, I, like a prisoner cut the days off one by one,
Waiting to be set free,
Waiting for your arrival,
Waiting for warmth,
Waiting for you.
On some days, I wish I could draw on your palm all the things
that you make me feel,
One by one.
They say people often turn into poets after they get their
hearts broken or when they're deep in love.
But am I a poet yet?
What do I write about?
The way the current runs through my ribs when I'm close to
you? Or after every heated argument the way my heart burns?
Or how I never loved dark brown eyes but yours remind me of
my favourite metropolis?
Or how, everyday I crave for your presence?
They say heartbreaks and love turn people into poets.
But baby, will you?
How I love the way our fingers move in a rhythm, like
honeybees dancing on summer afternoons
How your smile lights up the whole world as if you're my
sunlight on the darkest of days?
How, with every "I love you" every inch of me does the happy
dance.
How, every time you look at me, I'm on the verge of losing my
mind completely.
How on my dumb jokes you still laugh with every bit in your
body.
How you hate your laugh but that's one thing that keeps me

going.

How, whenever our song plays on the radio, I wish we were cuddled up in sheets.
How every millisecond with you is infinite.
How the scent of yours won't ever leave my mind even in a crowd full of people, searching you.
How bad I wish we could be together right now.
How bad I wish we don't end up being a story to tell.
How bad I wish I were curled up in the sheets with you and our fingers untwined and hearts racing.
How you are the forever that I wished for.
How all my 11:11 wishes would come true.

-Irenna Malik

hell of lust

In the sweet-smelling garden of lust,
Prancing like a jumbo bust,
Waiting by the lake for my host.
Attractive yet beauty at the most!

Through the silver-lined clouds came she.
Contempt, rising beats, a golden smile of glee.
Hosted the host, the golden queen,
"Hello! Bonjour, rejoice for what you have seen,
For you will witness the unseen.

Handcuffed by my sweetheart,
In what flaw knows no smart!
"Due what I die? What's my break?"
Sunken heart with a body of wreck.

"You will know," said the Goldie mail,
Reaching a heavy gate of golden rail.

Darkness thy should never encounter,
Like this was the jail of terror.

"Welcome again to the hell of lust,
Rejoice for living a life of rust,
Turmoil that you have lived inside
 The peace that you have left beside

Everything for a tomorrow of mend
Rule of Ancestors, rules for a bend?"

On the fire, below the rig,
Slipped down, lust a wig
Now in front of the sweetheart,
In what flaw knows only smart.

"Beg pardon, a poor prisoner of soil.
Hell leads now, life was a foil
Forgive me for a nose like that;
Hungry for the fulfilment, so that fat"

"Sure, not easy for any heart;
In what grace must know you smart.
Torn my mistakes, plastered by rules
Life a circus, but full of bulls!"

"Jump, dive, prance on your agility;
Need no endurance but brain's ability.
Hold tight the ropes of brain
Let the clouds of work make the rain.
Hard you work, better you drench
In the hell of lust, your thirst is quench!"

'From here, hear this say
For now, should leave no dismay!"
Kiss on cheek, relief on heart
Goodbye to sweetheart from this smart.

-Rahul Nayak

tunnel of life

There comes a phase in life when
The mind turns into a tunnel,
A tunnel that is filled with
Darkness, rage, solitude,
Anger, cynicism, gloominess.
Do not fall into that tunnel of sorrow,
Do not let that tunnel of hell swallow you,
Instead look, beyond the tunnel,
And try harder each day
To turn that tunnel of darkness
Into tunnel of light.
Seek light, seek glory, seek what you deserve.
Remember to fill that tunnel with
Laughter, joy, unconditional love,
Optimism, and amusement.
Things might be difficult now
But no matter what,
Survive,
Do not give up,
Keep fighting
And win the battle
In the Tunnel of Life!

-Padmini Peteri

love – before, after, always

Day even before, I fell in love-
When I saw her making her friends laugh,
As if spreading love and mirth, on God's behalf.
That moment, I knew, she was just the light I needed in my life,
I had to get to know her, make her my friend, lover, and one day, my wife.

Day before, I fell in love-
When she blushed and finally said "yes",
Her eyes expressing her joy more, her words less.
I had never been happier, young love consumed every inch of me,
Everything looked rosy, cozy, and easy, as far as my eye could see.

Day before yesterday, I fell in love-
When she turned red and yelled at me with rage,
Our relationship had moved from honeymoon period to the next stage.
I knew we had our share of problems, but after all, which couple did not?
After these ups and downs, I was sure we were going to reach a sweeter spot.

Yesterday, I fell in love-
When she showed the maturity to demand some time apart,
"It will only bring us closer," at least that's what I told my heart.
I kept trying my best to bring us back on track,

with wide open eyes

Little did I know she had left, only to never come back.

Today, I'm falling in love-
With how serene, joyous, and complete, by my own, I am.
And as I rejoice in myself, she just seems water over the dam.
For the first time, I'm free from the need to find joy in
someone else,
I feel like a wizard reborn, enchanted by my own spells.

Tomorrow, I will fall in love-
With the melody of birds, chirping in the early hour,
And the fluttering of butterflies, chasing each other from
flower to flower.
With the litter of puppies, biting and playing around,
Rollicking, frolicking, literally down to the ground.

Day after, I will fall in love-
With the grass grown in between the pavement blocks,
And the moss thriving on the little, damp rocks.
With the boundless blue sky, embellished by cottony white
clouds,
And the bounteous green planet, which it so lovingly shrouds.

Every moment now on, I'll keep falling in love-
With the gift of waking up to a new day every day and making
it come alive.
I now know, love's the journey and not the destination
It doesn't matter how long the drive.

-Saloni Wagle

lost

She was lost.
Lost in those silent dead streets,
surrounded by darkness
And her soul never felt so empty.
She never felt like this before.
She never felt that pain before.
Nobody understood the pain,
the pain of losing a mother.
She was lost.

Lost in the thoughts of her dead mother,
She wanted to run away from all this,
From the pain and from the mess in her life
With her bag full of memories
Of her dead mother.
She tried to keep the bag full of memories
Safely with her.
The bag of memories was the only thing
Which she never wanted to lose.
She left the house with that bag
And chose to never return.
She was lost.

-Prerna Agrawal

sacrifice

Peeking through the window, was one story,
Standing on the ground was another, and one far behind.
Which one to choose,
Sometimes, it was difficult to be wise.
One way led to her happiness,
Another to the happiness of those silent voices,
Unheard and unfelt, but louder and stronger.
She had left her everything for this day,
But she hadn't asked for it this way.

She knew what would give her eternal peace,
And then she saw the unheard voices meet.
That was bliss to her,
And to them, it was their world.

-Shreya Khemani

journey to me

When she will flower and in her very first glance,
Bud of the winter dew on lips grow,
She will cast her gaze towards the infinity.
And the veiled spring night
Of the tender full moon
With millions of star thriving,
Will be reflected upon.
She will whisper to the sleeping morning breeze,
Gone to address the assembly of the Angels!
Therefore, accepting an invitation from the fairies,
Flowing, surrounded by
And canopied by the sky
Of glory garnished by the millions
Of the divine artisans!

And now, she comes to the streams,
She shall swim.
She will listen to the divine birds of joyfulness
Singing the songs of the blissful souls
Giving her warmth when she's cold
Without him, she wouldn't be the same
When he hides behind clouds
She's gloomy
The sparkle in her eye.
The light in her life.
The purpose for thriving,
The cause for living.
The very generous and gentle,
The loveliest of them all.
Prowess of her glad grace,

Interrupting her gregariousness consuming perpetual
Carnival of her stars,
Her sharpness treasuring lucid and innocuous wild
Eyes,
With her pilgrim soul,
Trembling like glowing bars.

To make much of her streets wade
Through exquisitely delicate skies
She left smashed and twisted
To persist her prime,
Immaculately thrilled with a stonily look,
Rowing subtly to overcome her setback,
Amassing an immense content,
To merchandise her dreadful apparel with
Him.

-Uzlifat Zahoor

ashamed, no more

I am born with brown skin, dark with a glow,
But it was not funny to call me a crow.
I am chubby and stout, in a running race if I fall,
It hurt me to be named a rolling football.
I would dance alone in my room with a closed door,
Even if I participate in any group, I was chosen to ignore.
Growing up, I was still plump but became genetically tall,
With age, the nicknames changed, now I am a dinosaur.
I wanted to wear mamma's lovely gold earrings,
But aunty feels gold looks ugly on my dark skin.
I couldn't relish the dessert that looked yummy,
When a relative said, "Look! She has a tyre on her tummy."
One day, I felt, this is too much for my mind to follow,
I cried my heart out, shoving my face into the pillow.
Enough is enough, I am blessed with it and love my colour,
My rotund shape is better than your brainless skull.
On whatever beauty scale one can be ruling today,
Colours fade, shapes change, that is the rule of nature, my
friend.
Keep them in the drawers, whiteners are to cover a mistake.
I own this tan and I am going to have that cake.
I will wear the gold, I will eat what my mind delights,
Not the shape nor does skin bother, there is no more fright.
Healthy mind builds a healthy body,
To live happily, confidence within is the key.
I put on the red lipstick, get into that lovely dress,
When I look in the mirror, I don't care who else, but I am
impressed.

-Namita Das

the tales of my heart

Hear the tale of my broken heart,
I tried to take part,
To live and to believe,
To turn out to be a spear of integrity and verity.

Hopefully, I tried to hope, but hope is just an idea, a fleeting
thought, a wisp of optimistic bliss that I'm now too tired to
pursue with credibility.

All I await now is the warm hug of the soul reaper,
So I can go with a smile,
To a place away from unreliability.
I thought I had many friends
But I realized, none are mine.

This is the tale of my heart. I drift away, a ghost never there.
Never belonging, into nothingness I return,
Along with the skeletons who stare at me
With wide eyes and shocked spines.

-Mohammad Mudassir

promise to my beloved

My Promise To My Beloved

However vast the distance, I'll come for you;
Whatever resistance, I'll come for you.
I'll come for you
Because I have to say, my love,
that I love you.
I know that you are waiting for me,
And I'm longing for you, in my every sinew.
Though odds are high, and evens are few,
But I promise that I'll come for you.

If mountains fall, and jungles burn,
Quakes and storms are not a concern.
Typhoons, volcanoes can't stop my way,
Because I promised to you to return.

I want to see your smile, as fresh as dew,
So I promise, dear, that I'll come for you.

Slender thread of hope, I won't let it break,
Whatever happens, whatever it takes.
Take my words, I won't let you down.
I'll come for sure, whatever's at stake.
And here, my eyes are dying to see you, too
And I promise, love, that I'll come for you.

-Neha Prashar Verma

flawless night

O' night , you are the upheave of twilight,
You are quashing the light of day,
Clutching the regards of all livelihood
Through your dusky black cloth which reposes the entire
world.

There prevails utter silence...

The newcomers leisurely approaching,
The Moon – the Queen of night with its celestial gaze, alluring
Enchantment all over the shop...
Now, it's time for adornments.
The gleaming stars escort the Queen.
The shafts of the moon mirroring the lagoon!
The aura gives a pleasant breeze.

Gifted with a striking nativity of grandeur,
Ergo, sows the seeds of hush and love.

-Meenakshi Ramaswamy

a buddy to me

Many stiches in your entity,
The only veracious ones stay with certainty,
Indeed! It hardly has to be any,
In many...

Hunting for the right one may be nettled,
But to have one
Make you fully thrilled.

A good deed,
The very sole,
Out of ordinary,
That "who else" is your crony.

A friend to you is a priceless gift,
And you have lot to express,
But sadly, no gist
The feeling gets seized in you
But you enjoy the company of a few
The few are dreadful,
Important and soulful.

The only alms with no loss,
Thank you, God,
 For giving such premium gift across.

-*Vaishnavi Rajput*

because love is love

And she still loved him from a distance.

She didn't say, but that dried rose in her dairy did.
She smiled a lot, but her swollen eyes didn't.
She refused another love story, and her denial did.
She preferred vodka over mojito, and her choices did.
She went for solo drives to pacify herself, and her loneliness did.
She kept mum when needed to speak, and her silence did.
After he broke her heart into tiny million pieces, she didn't shout over or cry.
And yet, she loved him with all the broken pieces; that's where her power lay.

-Shikha Sharda

storms of you in me

There are storms of emotion inside me,
Trying to speak,
Will it end or will it collide,
Controlling me from within or
Subsuming me away with you?
Is it over time that I understood you?
Or is it just taking me long enough to completely understand
your absence away from me?
Your thought is unconsciously dreading away from the pain,
Or is it ripping it more?
Soulfully repeating it again,
My mind will continue living its process,
Apart or along with you.
Then question will rise:
Is it making me stronger, or weaker?
Without hesitating, it will say that loving you was always a
stronger truth.
So what upholds the mystery?
Will you end in me?
Your love will forever cease inside me!

-Divya Bora

conqueror: a tribute the acid attack victims

You are beautiful the way you are.
No marks or stain could define your soul.

You are a warrior, we are proud so far.
Don't bother about those cotton stoles.

My dear, it's not you who should hide.
The culprit ashamed should have cried.

Your pain, your loss is not measurable,
But believe me, all our hearts are understandable.
Yes, we can't get the wrong done right,
But allow us to comfort your pain and turn the dark into a day
bright.

Please believe us, we apologize.
Get your feathers back and energize.
You are meant to fly.
You can and will reach the sky.
We salute the conquerors.

You taught us to live and smile as fighters.
Just remember – You are precious and beautiful the way you
are.

-The Wanderer Mind

i killed my love

What I did was what they told me, not my mind at work
Those procedures felt more robotic than conscious.
Do my choices define me? No, as I made none.
It's a power possessed by those hands, not mine.
It's either this or that, like nickel and dime.
They say its love, but I know not what's true
As I felt nothing of it, senselessly following rules.

I'm not happy how we met, unwilling to budge
You had lots to say unlike me, so I let you sway,
Not my consort or counsel, yet so out of control
You bite the hand that fed you, a mad dog in ways.
Forget the tragedy that followed, me trusting you
You defined love for me, to you I pinned my heart,
They told me I'd be sorry, so I chose to break free.
Regret flooding in now, karma has finally found me.

Their bonds to me shattered, I came home to you.
But in your arms stood instead, another distressed damsel,
Smothered by your affection, embracing the devil's kiss.
What was I to you then, for whom did I leave?
The family that raised me, the master who fed?
You put the blame on my change, and I beg to differ
You were my cup of hemlock, destruction bound to be.

Yet, you are not my reason, but my beloved excuse
To find freedom from restraints, they never set for me.
How can I go back to them, how may I explain,
The love that I had sought for was with them indeed?
Their love to me was their not-so-light commands,

with wide open eyes

Violently murdered by my ignorant acts
All that I can do now is to carry out its coffin,
To follow this lamented love, to my eternal bliss.

-Nirosha Tomy

anxietas

How long does a good day last?
What kind of attachment do I have from the past?
When will the next beautiful day show itself?
Why is the room getting smaller like a shelf?

You have to tell me if there is a medicine
Because my mind is filled with bad adrenaline
I imagine and I think of thoughts I wish I don't own
I have a feeling that my organs are made of bone.

I don't know where all this blood is coming from
But the red streak slowly crawls downward like a worm
I feel it creeping like a centipede's hundred legs

Please stare at my eyes and observe how it begs.
Anxiety is looking at the mirror and seeing your skeleton
Watching your skull shiver as it chatters and grinds its teeth
Seeing, expecting, waiting for you to fall apart.

There are lines on the ground that point everywhere
I don't know why it did not start from me at all
The lines only multiply and direct me everywhere
I don't know if I should follow any of them at all.

Tell me, what to do?
But don't tell me to leave my shelf.
Tell me, what to say?
But don't let me speak too much.
How do I stop thinking?
How do I stop waiting?

with wide open eyes

Why do I keep on shaking?
Why should I keep on waking?
Why should I...

-Earljanne Ofalla

like the light of a guiding star

When I was lost, and the light was gone,
When the darkness engulfed, and I started to sob,
My days just passed, and the nights were long,
Full of fears and pain and hurt.

When I started to think it was all my fault,
When my beliefs faded and I couldn't hold,
You entered my life, like the light of a guiding star.
The star so bright, that shined with the might,
Who took away the slightest of plight.

The one who cared and took me to surprise,
The one who loved and told me to shred the fright.
You dove inside the deepest of my eyes
And paved the way to inspiration of my life.

And then, the day came when darkness overruled.
I fretted and dreaded and tears started to pool.
I tossed and turned every stone for the clue.
I screamed and cried but
There was no you!

Near the horizon, the light twinkle again,
A drop of hope trickled down again,
I ran and begged to hold me tight
Only to realize it's the mirage of the mind.

with wide open eyes

Then I heard the sound, the sound of you
Calling out, "Inside you, look!"
It's when I found that it's the light to dread
For the darkness is what that always dwells!

-Shivani Kaushik

saving grace

I know the agony is barraging your heart,
tearing memories apart,
Kindled spirit rushing to escape, a breather you tryna chase'
Don't stray away to a cage human, we don't house weakness;
I promise...
People are worth exploring than places,
Secrets wrapped in layers, treasured in gold cases.
They could be a lot of things, which lens are you wearing?
Keep your eyes wide open
to the possibilities yet to come,
Comb the courage to harbour their embrace,
Eschew prodding the sacred ground, your mental space.
Honey, glance at the mirror just once,
Right there is your saving grace.

-Deepesha J.

thought of you

Just the thought of you passing by
Fills my stomach with butterflies,
What were the odds we could've met,
Now that I know you, I'll never forget.

The thought of your smile that's so cute,
Lifts up my heart, yet makes me mute,
Love isn't something I've already known,
Now even in a crowd, I feel alone.

Just the thought of meeting you again
Brings me joy and relieves the pain.
Life feels tough when we are apart,
Now distance does matter though connected by heart.

A thought of you would do anything,
Happiness and pain at once it brings,
Even if we aren't meant to be together,
I'm happy our paths crossed once, for the better.

-Jagruthi Kommuri

promise

Even when the skies go dark,
The storm strikes its spark.
Walking through the sand,
I'll never leave your hand.
On our journey, patches may go rough,

Times may go tough,
Together we'll walk this road
And find our way home.
What may bring tomorrow,

We'll build our Reich together
I promise you a smile, my Queen,
A smile forever.

-Abhishek Kulkarni

sometimes

Sometimes, we let go of the things we love,
We make mistakes, we fall, we lie above.
Sometimes, we try hard to make life perfect,
We realize, we apologize, after we regret.

Sometimes, we feel life will fall into place,
We try harder than we could, just to match the pace.
Sometimes, we are helpless and tired of trying,
We sit back and hope, life will be worth living before dying.

Sometimes, we smile when we are dead inside,
We force it, which leads to a misguide.
Sometimes, we are fed up and want all this to end,
We break the barriers and become weak to bear life's bend.

Sometimes, we want things so badly,
We make an effort to achieve it exactly.
Sometimes, we are left with unaccomplished dreams,
We lay emotionless in tears with silent screams.

-Najam Us Saher

progress

That little step you stumble to take,
That decision you doubt to make.
That weakness you try to overcome,
Will be the strength of what you become.

Try a little harder one more time,
When it's time, stars do shine.
It might not be success yet,
It is progress, you'll win, I bet,
Cause mistakes does not define success,
Success is the process of how you progress.

-Jagruthi Kommuri

not strangers

83

We pass by like strangers
Putting on a façade,
But we both
Remember.

-Inkforyou

of making a house your home

Maybe love isn't about change,
Maybe it's about falling for each other
Just the way they are.
It's sort of like
Moving into a new house.
At first,
You're too much in love with all the perfections
And can't believe all this belongs to you.
And a while down the lane
You start loving it
For its little scrapes and scratches
For the little broken parts
For all the things that are wrong,
You know it so well.

You know how to open doors
Without making a noise,
Or which floorboards creak a little.
You know how to unlock the stuck lock
On a cold Monday morning.
And
Maybe
That's all that really matters.
To love
For more than perfection.

-*Sukti Sisodiya*

his favorite book

His favorite book,
Was the one that he knew every word to.
Wet fingers smearing the words,
But it didn't matter because he re-read each chapter
So many times that he could recite each page by heart.
The bind beginning to become undone from folding the cover
back,
The corners of each page left unfinished folded neatly and
tucked in to remember where he had left off the last time he
read.
His favorite parts highlighted in gold
And he smiled whenever he came across them.
But eventually, even your favorite things become old.
You replace them with a newer version.
A better story.
A flawless cover.

Fresh pages for you to learn.
What once was considered to be full of magic,
Is now just a worn-out object
Collecting dust in a bookshelf
And only kept because it was once
Too valuable
To throw out—
I used to be his favorite book.

-Liz Amsel

pleasant morning

The nature has awoken;
And so have I
My dreams have broken,
And here I lie.
The night has ended, giving me a warning,
And invited me to admire this pleasant morning.

Golden rays, of sunshine,
So warm and tender,
Kiss the dew drops and the grass,
Into morning, sunrise surrenders.

A flight of colourful butterflies,
So light and enchanting.
Absorbs the aroma of the flowers,
Diffuses the scent in this morning.

The chirping of birds,
So melodious and soothing.
It compels me to wake up
To admire this morning.

Sunshine finds its way towards me,
Colourful butterflies touch me,
The birds sings in my ears,
It is nature that I hold dear.

-Najam Us Saher

survival

To the caged wings,
To the vanished peace,
To the enslaved dreams,
To the missed opportunities,
To the lost smile,
To the shallow eyes,
To the darkest days,
To the life that ceases to exist,
To the encaged voice,
To the faded spirit,
To the entangled life,
You will get back your wings to fly,
Until then, survive!

-Padmini Peteri

the colours of love

In the colours of love, there is a purple heart,
whence you delve into the colours of love,
and your mind, soul and spirit opens anew.

The world stands in awe before your powerful presence.
You have become enlightened,
fresh dreams are flowing;
you have been given a new life, a new clue.

It doesn't matter if you're a traveller, a beggar or King
Love entrances all, no matter which world
or generation you belong to.
Love is incomprehensible.

When you wear the cloth of love,
the ground becomes a bed of flowers.
The world bows before you. This is love.
It is a feeling of grandeur. That is unsensible.

The people do not matter
The colour of love blinds all
but makes you see clearer than ever before.
This is the colour of love.

-Mohammed Mudassir

when the winter falls

You collect so many years
From the garden of life,
Overcoming all your fears.

Forget about the thorns
Let the blood drool
Stay grim and forlorn.

Call it okay to miss a few hours
Of pleasure rain
Wait, till it next time showers.
But will it again?
Make sure.
Will it have pleasure to attain
'Cause when the winter falls,
You will miss everything.
You will miss every little drizzle
As no one will hear,
To your frozen calls.

-Sarvani Sita

hope

I tried to stomp out
The hope
That was tearing me apart,
Only to realize
It was also keeping me
Alive.

-Inkforyou

never give up

When you are upset,
I will bring back your smile.
When you are tired,
I'll walk with you every mile.
Tilts or fights
Nothing can divide,
Beyond the rights and wrongs
I'll always be by your side.
You are my midnight muse,
Beautiful sunshine,
Seven colours spectrum
My blush wine.
If you are lost in thought,
I'll give you all my love
To revive your smile, gorgeous,
Remember I'll never give up.

-Abhishek Kulkarni

before it's too late

Feelings are many, feelings are real,
They are sometimes painful to deal,
Many you wish to share,
But only few who care;
Feelings you hide deep within the heart,
You try to speak out as you struggle to start.
A 'sorry' left too long,
'I love you' untold.
'Thank you' that's unsaid,
A 'goodbye' you wish was told.

Feelings concealed and truths that you hold,
Are to be revealed, before death may unfold.
'Cause you never know if life would ever wait
 So, speak out the secret before it's too late.

-Jagruthi Kommuri

hope

A small word with deep meaning is hope,
The power that supports you through life's steep slope.

The power that will not only make you grateful for what you
have now,
But will also be the answer to your each and every 'how'.

It will make you believe in 'the brighter tomorrows',
The tomorrows with more joys and lesser sorrows.

It will teach you that nothing is the end,
That there's no harm in standing out; you don't always have to
blend.

It will show you how believing in yourself can work magic,
It will show you the solutions to every tragic happening.

The power that you should have in times of good and bad,
When you're happy, when you're sad.

Once you possess hope, don't keep it to yourself,
Spread it from person to person and let it help everyone to
find a better version of themselves.

-Disha Shinde

frame me in your heart

For if I could be the colour on your canvas,
I would never be a soul so colourless.
Brush me like the indigo hues of a dark sky,
Or like the free birds soaring high.

Just as the shades of pink you colour,
A thousand strokes of perfection to the water.
Strike me along like the reflection,
Or like the setting sun in the horizon.

Along the seas you create the mountains,
Darkest brown brush of the colour makes a chain.
Create, me too, like a picture of a tale,
Or like the boat that alone sails.

Paint me like a picture in your heart,
Discover my admiration for thee like an art.
Remember me like the shades of your colour,
Or like a secret admirer yet to discover.

-Najam Us Saher

i am tired

Strongest warriors have the toughest battles, they say, trying to
give some comfort,
But what if that badge of honour does not outshine the hurt?

What if I am tired to take this any forward,
What if I have more than enough suffered,
And can no longer hold on to my record?

What if I am done keeping my voice covered,
What if my future does seem to be a desert,
Having had enough lessons from life learnt?

What if so much injustice life did offer,
What if things are all blur and unclear,
And I can no longer handle it like a master?

What if I am tired of always being alert,
What if those words seem to me absurd,
And no longer as a warrior I wish to be referred?

What if I am tired to keep my mind in divert,
What if to a vulnerable child I wish to revert,
And to be that strong warrior I no more covet?

What if life's truth I have already uncovered,
But from the wounds I will never be recovered?
I know I sound like a lost coward,
With spirit and head lowered,
But what if I really am exhausted and tired?

-*Madhurya Kommuri*

pride ruins

Your heart so wide,
Shrunk to an ant's hole all because of pride.
Sure it is a high tide,
But is it a fruitful ride?

You hold on to it so tight,
And miss little things that give delight.
You might think it gives you might,
But a life with pride is a never-ending fight.

Good will be vanished,
Future all tarnished,
Success will be diminished.
Inside, if you let it reside,
You are destroyed once and for all.
Give it a thought and decide,
Is it really worth the fall?

-*Madhurya Kommuri*

beautiful

Words fail me time and again
Your beauty is beyond their contain
With you, I am me,
You are the reason I want 'to be'.
You are the river flooding my soul,
Your touch makes me whole,
You warm my heart,
Girl, let our story start.

-Abhishek Kulkarni

sleepless nights

Those were the beautiful nights,
When they were endless for us.
Where nights changed into days,
But we hardly cared.
But then the time changed.
Where now the nights haunt,
Where your memories are endless.
Where still the nights change to day
But now who hardly cares.

-Sushma Chaudhary

love-hate

Love comes naturally from birth,
It's hatred that we are taught on this earth,
Love isn't complex to understand,
It's not confined to one —it expands.

Love is everywhere, if you see,
It's our vision that's blurred and obscure.
Love is within us, even if you don't agree,
It's just we are so arrogant to accept that we are not pure.

Love is found in every person's heart,
It is hate that's keeping humans apart,
One doesn't need to learn how to love,
It's how we are created naturally by God above.

-Jagruthi Kommuri

i heal

Trying to forget the sorrows, my heart, I seal
Ruptured emotions of my ruthless life, I conceal,
Passion and concern from the one who loves me, I feel,
After years of tormented life, finally, I heal.

Rage vanished and anger dissolved,
Situations changed and heart resolved,
Life gave me a chance; it absolved,
After years of patience, Love evolved.

Negative thoughts faded as confusion,
Sadness left me and ended my seclusion,
I find myself happy and away from isolation,
At last, I hope I feel excluded from depression.

Everything appears blissful and pleasing,
I find my love for you increasing,
Sadness to happiness my feelings are replacing,
Happy I am, I find myself healing.

Your acceptance, I encounter,
You made me feel beautiful as a flower,
You I want to empower,
Love upon you, I shower.

I wish to be with you in every phase,
I promise to never part ways,
I hope I brighten your days,
I pray, love keep us together always.

-Najam Us Saher

love

Love has been defined by many,
Nevertheless we always contradict in some or the other way,
Every person might've loved someone so deep,
Yet have lost love 'cause they couldn't dare to convey.

Do they not say love gives us strength?
Then why is it that we are weak to show?
They say love will come back if it's meant,
But why do we test love, only to let it go?
If pain is the result of love,
Isn't everyone in pain?
If heartbreak is what we have to survive,
Isn't love worth the wait for the gain?
If waiting means your love is true,
Isn't everyone waiting till eternity?
If only we could win love,
By enduring life's austerity.

-Jagruthi Kommuri

she

She shined brightly,
Like the sun.
Her beauty was exuberant
That could be compared to the flowers.
Her smile was so infectious,
That it made a sad person smile.
Her smile could never be caged;
She flew high like the birds,
Flying higher with each passing day.
She made friends and stuck to them;
She inspired people,
Loved by many,
And hated by none.
She was her family's pride,
Helpless people's savior.

But behind that infectious smile,
Did anyone see the pain?
The torture her thoughts put her in, every day.
Those sleepless nights, filled with constant tears,
Yet she pulled herself up each day,
And smiled again like she was the happiest soul.
But she knew what lay beneath her smile,
Sorrow, anguish, worthlessness.
She was caged by her thoughts,
By her loneliness, by her everlasting sadness,
And she did not know the reason behind her sadness,
She had all the love and comfort one needed
She had everything she ever dreamt off,
And yet she wanted none of it,

with wide open eyes

All she wanted was to die calmly,
Yet she survived each day patiently.

-*Padmini Peteri*

when i become a shell

These days, I can feel my heartbeat
At the bottom of my shoes.
Because I am treading on
Everything that is keeping me alive.
I can't look anyone in the eye.
Maybe it is the guilt I feel from existing, simply
Or the fright I want to hide
That rushes forth so swiftly,
Even when I swear that it is concealed.
Even poetry refuses to keep being my shield.
I am stripped bare,
Raw.
Left as an example for my own self:
This is what you should not have become.

-A'Danya Blake

we will unite again

You under the ground, and me above,
The sand slipping through my fingers.
Your cold gravestone is my warmest place,
 Surely, we will unite again.

-Tugce Gokoglu

i will stop loving you

I will stop loving you
Once you have counted
Every raindrop
That has fallen tonight.

-Tugce Gokoglu

contrast

I was enticed by your strength,
But you called yourself weak.

I was drawn to your kindness,
But you said you were cruel.

I fell for your understanding,
But you barely understood yourself.

-Inkforyou

exposed

The only part of me I have ever undressed,
For anyone,
Is my mind.
I was still beautiful
Even that naked.
Even so bare.
I was the light that needed to stay on.

-A'Danya Blake

it's three o' clock again

It's three o' clock again.
You shuffled your playlist while talking to the posters and the
immortal words.
A force was dragging you underneath the blanket,
Supernatural happenings were far beyond from existence.
You had believed in underlying truths about metamorphosis
of the leaves,
You shed last night and reformed anew.
Days had been solitary to nights.
There seemed no difference, but the rush for the seconds.
Suddenly, it struck four.
Eyes were known and trembled,
When the doorbell rang.
There was no human, left for solace.
Time had played its part.
She could see the grey movements, hallucinations invincible.
4 am thoughts were drearier.
3 am brought no Goth,
Shadows of nothing compelling her.
To leave an open letter
of denial.
The fish was out of the water, it seemed,
Breaths would last for seconds, thoughts would scream purple.
Shadows were consuming her when she unfolded her arms.
Glanced at her diary,
She decided to fight.
She decided to be back!

-Tejasvee Nagar

stardust

My subconscious mind borrowed
Some of the pearled stardust,
While he narrated the dreams
From his cosmic combust.

Following his imprints,
I tripped over the moon,
To land on a galaxy
Surreal, but unknown.

As I caught his sight,
He expressed surprise.
After all, the dream was his
Which I had just trespassed!

Walking through
The starry paths, so divine!
He pointed the stars
Which he believed would align.
To drive love into
Our hearts once intertwined.

Suddenly, the radiance
Of the moon started fading.
I clutched his hand
Sensing the dream was ending.

Take me back to the galaxy
Just once before I rise,
This time, for me to
Only see those stars align!

-*Swetha Nair*

about her

Mother, I've got something to tell you about her,
Daddy, Swear to God I will never find another.
If you let me, I can show you what she's made of,
Trust me, she will never be another turnoff.

Please, be kind to her when I take her home,
If you're rude, please kindly leave her alone.
She's the sweetest thing that ever happened to me,
A life with her is all that I wanted to see.

Mother, don't let me kneel down and beg,
Baby, I've got something to tell you about her.
She's my mother, and I don't want to find another.
She won't let us be alone and live together,
She just wanted to find someone who is greater.

Darling, I know I love you, but I love her more,
She resides in my heart, in the middle of the core.
She had told me things to become a better man,
I want to please her to the very best I can.
Baby don't let me kneel down to you and beg.

-Earljanne Ofalla

captivated

And on one starry night like this
The immeasurable beauty of the sky
What a pity
I couldn't enjoy it
Or adore its beauty.
Because in front of me
Stood you
Far more wonderful
And bright
And lovely
That the sky seemed to struggle
To catch up with your immeasurable beauty.
Little did it know,
Its struggle would go waste
Because your soul has captivated my eye
In a way
Nothing
Absolutely nothing else can
—loving far and beyond, deep into the ocean of the eye.

-Sukti Sisodiya

flailing, fighting

You say I'm awesome,
You say I'm great,
You say you don't deserve me,
And yet you ignore me.

I count the minutes till you respond,
Minutes turn into hours thus far,
Why expect me to grow and love,
To shed my fears and my painful past,
When you're the one that's
Pushing me down, kicking
My knees out from under me?

Offering me an arm to lean on,
Then pulling away even before I can stand.
I'll stumble and break, I know.
How well you know that, too.
But you're still doing it.
I wish I had the strength to punch you back,
At least then you'd know how much it hurts.

Starting with a sweet message in the morn
No response to my replies till noon
And even then, ignoring the text
That matters the most to me.
I still keep on, more texts at 1
You reply at 9, monosyllabic to the end.
I might write a hate-filled poem
I might decide to hold a grudge
I might want to hate you,

To not trust you, to walk away
But I just can't, how much ever I try.

I can't keep my distance,
I still can't help hoping
Even now my mind says,
"What if I'm wrong?
What if I'm overreacting?
What if I'm just a jealous bitch?"

I don't know what to think anymore.
All you did was help me up,
Just to make me slip and fall.
I trusted you so very much
I think I still do.
I've told you I'm naïve
But never did I expect to be so wounded.

I walked into the lake
Of my own accord, knowing well
The possibilities and the consequences.
I thought you'd be the one
To help me out, but now,
I know you'll let me drown.

You know, this isn't the first time,
And it certainly won't be the last.
I'm more loving than you know
I'm more clueless than you think
But I'm also kinder than most.
I've dealt with more pain than I show.

Which is very hurtful.
I chose to trust you,

To love you,
It's my own fault.
I have no one to blame
There is no one else to hate
It's just anxiety right now.
Other for you
I'll make it back up, without you.
I'll stand on my feet, steady and strong
I can't say you led me on.
It was my own heart that
Convinced me to hope.
Leave me alone.

For I'm a catastrophe.
You've left me a bleak abyss.
The stories of my past once again
Ring true, now it proves that I must
Learn from my mistakes, my past.
Leave me alone.
For you know, I cannot.
Let me be, let me hurt.
There's nothing more you can do now.

I could hope that I misunderstood,
But I know the ways of the world too well.
No one will ever hold on
As tight as I always do.
Fret not, dear "friend",
I'll pull myself out soon enough.
I may be naïve, I may be a kid
But I'm stronger than you think
I've faced more than you've seen.

-Uthra Baskaran

You

I don't want to write today.
I don't want to construe your incentives.
I don't want to remind myself of your chiseled edges and carved countenance.
I don't want to recall the anamnesis of when you would squeeze my hand tighter, while your dagger would go in deeper.
So while I open this box of memories, I try to deflect the emotions that attempt to crawl up my skin and possess it.
You once told me that you would like to paint my face.
Make my lips golden yellow, like the glow emanating from my soul.
You wanted to sketch tiny florets on my eyelids which would bloom in their own time, just like the stories persisting on my waterline.
The rest of my face would be filled with poetic lines, which were naturally etched on my heart.
Colors always fascinated you.
Love was red, sorrow was blue, and anger was black.
You never had a color for heartbreak, for your heart was covered in band aids but not sutures.
So what color did you see when you pulled the dagger out and turned your back on me?
Your artistry knew no bounds.
Like a meticulously planned masterpiece, you erased my beliefs with a snap of your fingers.
Now that you're gone, will my words carry the same ardour?
Will they still send shivers down your spine and transfix you?
Will they help deliver those unsung songs resting on my tongue?

Maybe they won't, maybe they never will.
I still don't want to write today.

-Preeti Kale

isolation of the mind

My sights,
Desperately search for lights
'Cause in the hours of the night,
My nightmares are so bright.
A part of me was missing
As he left the world for no reason.
I was four-cornered
But denied the pang of concern.

It hurt
And I couldn't make it stop.
There was pain
With no gain.
No tears crossed my mind
But my fears weren't kind.

A loss so great
With terms I couldn't accept.
So I ran away
And hid in my subconscious.

My body was present
But my mind was absent.

I felt safe
With my feelings caged,
It was my only escape route.
Time passed
But I was trapped.
I had detached my sanity

From what was left of my humanity.
My emotions were permanently separated.
The damage was done,
And I knew it.

My pesky feelings in isolation
Was my only solution.

-Abby Kayy

midnight fairy

I lay on my bed
Eyes glued at the clock,
Needles spurn even to attempt a shiver,
Mystically stuck, at 11:11!

"Make a wish dear!"
I heard the midnight fairy whisper.

My mind played a montage of all those wishes
That I wasted on the shed eyelashes,
Fueled well with pain yet failed to take off,
As it endured, in its wings,
The weight of my sorrows.

I could manifest the midnight fairy,
Silently escape through my window,
Because just as I shut my eyes to try my luck,
The clock betrayed resuming its tickle.

Heaving a sigh I moved my eyes
From the clock to the sheer curtain
That softens the moonlight entering my room,
Painting everything blue,
My emotions too!

-Swetha Nair

confusion

The road ahead seemed straight and flat,
The steep and curves were a stunning surprise.
The borders vanished between fiction and fact,
Chaos and confusion began to reprise.

The goals, once clear, are now blurred vision.
Rapidly deterring from my mission.

Withheld my ability to reason,
To fathom this uncanny phenomenon.

All around seems upside down,
Feels like a stranger out of town.

Everything so difficult to make whole,
As I transition to a deranged soul.

-Midhun B M

empty glass

I poured myself out to you
I thought you were parched
But it came back out
Through the holes
In your heart;
The holes punctured through
With betrayal
And lies
And so my love for you
Fell onto the floor
Wasted
And the glass you poured me
Was empty.

-Inkforyou

acknowledgements

Special thanks must go to the entire team of Inkfeathers Publishing who helped me out throughout the entire process of finding writers and compiling their beautiful poems into this book. Thanks a lot for giving me this golden opportunity and making this wonderful dream possible.

I want to thank my amazing authors whose constant love and support helped me to create this book. I'm eternally grateful to Vivek Kushwah for reaching out to me with this opportunity. To Tanishk Singh for his kind help and support throughout the process.

To my family, mostly my father for inspiring and supporting me every single day. To my friend Rutuja Dighe for helping me out with the editor's note. I'd also like to express my gratitude to my brother for his valuable advice and support.

And to all of my readers and poetry lovers for showering a book with love.

With love,
Deepali Giri
Compiler

meet the
co-authors

with wide open eyes

Paola Mora

Paola Mora is a 21-year-old law student from Mexico that aspires to be a human rights lawyer and make a change in today's society, making everyone understand that we are all the same and should be treated like it. She loves writing poetry that makes people feel heard and acknowledged, so that they know they are not the only ones going through something.

Luna Adair

Luna Adair is budding poet. Her poems often describe the strengths of self-love, as well as the theme of love, heart breaks and the spirit of wild youth. Through her poems she illuminates how magic of words takes us to a completely different world and at the same time makes the reader relate with them. She aims to give them  something to remember and hold onto. Luna shares her work on Instagram with her followers.

A'Danya Blake

A'Danya considers that she did not even know she could write poetry until she simply did, out of need. It became a therapeutic way to cope with her own emotions. In writing, with no formal training, she lends herself heavily to emotional expression, and considers everything else secondary. Her sole wish for her work is that it coaxes people to give in to their own emotions and feel something.

Midhun BM

Never too busy for vast seas and night skies, Midhun B M is a final year engineering student and a poet by passion. Born in Thiruvananthapuram, Kerala, he lived at various places in India. His taste for writing was first recognized by one of his primary school teachers. Later he went on to write several poems as gifts for his beloved and on several online platforms.

Jarod Wabick

P Jarod is a 34-year-old from Buffalo, NY. He enjoys the corner bar, bookstores, antique shops, music, and writing. Jarod found his voice in the written word in middle school when he first started writing ghost stories, then song lyrics, short stories and eventually poetry where he has felt most comfortable and in-tune. Jarod plans to use poetry as an outlet for as long as the words let him. This is his escape, his tranquillity, and his passion.

Liz Amsel

Liz Amsel graduated from an American University with a degree in English. She recently branched out and started sharing her poetry online and is excited to be a part of her first anthology! She is in the process of writing other works as well, such as short stories and has even started writing a novel.

Ann Chaiti Sarkar

Ann Chaiti Sarkar is a senior-school English teacher by profession. She loves writing poetry, fictional short stories, and factual ones too. Writing ingenuously has always allowed herself to appear as a silhouette in her fictions, where her characters borrow her emotions and enact it on paper. She had started writing at a very young age and the first poem she had ever written was a poem dedicated to her late grandpa. A life without writing would be null and void, her only way of escapism from this mundane and chaotic world would cease to exist. Once in a while everyone needs to get away and elude from scuffle, so writing for her is that unicorn at the end of the rainbow, that respite and intermission in the stage we call life.

Annapurani Vaidyanathan

She is a 27-year-old mad hatter who can wolf down packets of M&M's before you bat your eyelids. She is an Instrumentation Engineer, Author, Poet, and Blogger. She will lay her life down for Roger Federer. She is passionate about technology, art, culture, and literature. Her poetry has been published in various journals including Safety, The Literary Yard, and In Frame magazine. She loves working with numbers and hoards books for a living. Presently, she is a financial journalist.

Uthra Baskaran

An enthusiastic reader, Uthra finds solace from the complexities of everyday life within fiction. She expresses herself through her writing, and usually uses poetry as her medium. She's an introvert who loves getting to know people, but books will remain her closest friends. She treasures the classics and anything that makes her smile. She believes that a smile, even a forced one, can brighten your day, and someone else's too.

Sukti Sisodiya

Sukti Sisodiya is an aspiring poet and illustrative artist. She writes on the genres love, hope and heartbreak. She runs an advice column on Instagram. She is deeply interested in biology, psychology, music, and art. She is an intersectional feminist. You can connect with her on Instagram @poetrybysukti.

Earljanne Ofalla

Earljanne is a trainer in a BPO company. He wants to be an educator and a full-time writer. He has a degree in Sociology and is highly interested in studying philosophy. He plans to try and experience different art forms like music and video. He aspires to someday write the stories of the marginalized to share their plights.

Isheta Boruah

Isheta Boruah, the 20-year-old writer, hails from Assam, Guwahati. Apart from writing she also has a keen interest in legal aspects and has interned and put her hands-on sectors encircling Human Rights, Intellectual Property Rights, Criminal and Civil Law, and has also wrote and published Research Papers pertaining to Human Rights facets. She is currently pursuing BA. LLB Honours from National Law University and Judicial Academy, Assam. She is also working as an Editor for of Magazine and E-newspaper. She also has experience in swimming and has bagged laurel encircling the area.

Sarvani Sita

Her name is Sarvani. She is a flexible writer pouring her thoughts and feeling into words. She wants her poems to reach masses and enrich their perceptions about various matters. She is a versatile writer with undeniable passion and tenacity. She wishes to see a better tomorrow for the future generations. She is also a medical aspirant. You can connect with her on Instagram @poetryphobic.

Akshay Rathore

P Akshay, who goes by the pen name of Eerav, writes about mental health issues, romance, and mysticism, and is trying to make the world a better place through his poetry.

Preeti Kale

A 20-year-old wandering soul stuck in a unicorn's body, well that's what she wishes she were. She enjoys painting skies purple with her words, while her eyes are closed, humming away to another soft ballad. She's a faithful binge watcher and avid reader. Surrounded by medical books all day, she turns to writing as an outlet and therapy. Someday, she hopes her writing will mean something to someone.

Inkforyou

Poet and overthinker who writes about love, heartbreak, beauty, and life.

Yukti Arya

She's an amateur writer and artist, currently exploring her strengths. Yukti has been writing over a year now. She is always interested in writing about the human emotions.

Shikha Sengar

Busy around office chaos during the day and sleeping through poetries at night. Her poems are usually a survival guide for broken things and broken people. Also, she is extremely proud of her only treasure in the world, her enormous collection of books.

Juwairiyah Tariq Sayeed

A high school senior, Juwairiyah Tariq Sayeed, loves penning poetries and flash fiction. She derives inspiration from the wondrous beings hidden in the by-lanes and heart touching occurrences she comes across. She transfigures emotions into beautiful words, speaking to the world through the ink. She can be found on Instagram @flight_of_words.

Abby Kayy

Abby Kayy is a law student at the prestigious Nigerian university, Obafemi Awolowo University. She is an aspiring lawyer, poet and writer who hopes the world gets a chance to read her works. She's successfully written a teen fiction on Wattpad and Web novel and hopes to write more fiction works in the nearest future. She strives to be better at what she does and hopes to take her writing to another level.

Dazima Rai

Dazima Rai is a resident of Nepal and this is the first time she has published her poem in a book.

Najam Us Saher

Najam Us Saher is a B.A graduate from Hyderabad. Her poetry is a blend of expressions of hopelessness and yet being hopeful about the future. Her words are a true reflection of the way she lives her life and her transformation on emerging as a stronger girl than before. Her poetry does not rhyme always but is tuned with your hearts once you connect to her words.

Abhishek Kulkarni

Abhi is a poet, hobby writer and traveller. He loves to express emotions in the form of poetry and blog about his travel experiences. He likes to explore life to the fullest. His inspiration has been nature, his personal experiences and road trips. He has been collecting his poems over 5 years now.

Sushma Chaudhary

Sushma Chaudhary, a girl who got the eyes of innocence, the face of an angel, a personality of a dreamer and a smile that hides more pain than one ever can imagine. She has been an educator for five years. She loves to get lost in the world of imagination just by reading novels. She finds her second home in the books and makes herself feel more comfortable when she writes, and it unburdens her mind. Her writing can be found on her Instagram @its__me0602 as Deseo. She is writing her own story and hopefully she will publish her book soon.

Madhurya Kommuri

Madhurya, is an aspiring psychologist by profession and a poet by passion. A perfect imperfection, a beautiful mess is what defines her the best. Bringing out the stories people bury inside with patience and comforting with soothing poetry is her little way of bringing peace to minds and making world a better place for lives.

Alka Prakash

Alka Prakash, started writing as a hobby when she was 12. Wattpad was the place when she felt connected to writing and since then it has been an inevitable part of her. Currently she is a class 12th student from Jharkhand, India.

Tugce Gokoglu

Tugce Gokoglu, a 19-year-old student from the Netherlands, began her poet journey about a year ago by creating @amarpoetry on Instagram. Amar Poetry is about feelings and emotions that cannot easily be expressed verbally. These sentiments are delicately put into words, with the hope to help and inspire other. Sensitive topics such as love, pain and death are conveyed in small sentences, yet with large meaning.

Shivani Kaushik

A software engineer by profession but an artist by passion. An ordinary girl with an extraordinary spirit to learn and expand the realms of knowledge. Someone who as an artist, loves to paint what she can't express in words and loves to write what she can't express on canvas!

Tejasvee Nagar

She is a wanderer in this word land, that is who she is. Tejasvee Nagar, a 17-year-old living through the ink. The poetry which tears her apart makes her live, that is what poetry has been for her. You can leave the reviews for her poems if you wish at nagartejasvee@gmail.com

Snehal Agarwal

Snehal Agarwal is a 21-year-old Chartered Accountant from Mumbai. She is talkative, a sitcom fanatic and secretly a nerd. Her stories are a reflection of events commonly occurring around us yet ignored by most. She believes in making a change in the society, one day at a time.

Irenaa Malik

Irenaa Malik is a poet, writer, and a passionate reader. Her poetry comes straight from her heart, she finds peace and solace in it. She strongly believes in "what you seek is seeking you". She identifies herself as a feminist and hopes to bring a change around her through her write ups.

Rahul Nayak

Rahul Nayak, a student who is currently pursuing his bachelor's degree loves writing stories that are close to his heart. He started writing about 4 years ago and is currently working on his debut novel. He has an eminent appetite for movies and hence, his works are a visual treat in themselves. He believes, "Romance exists in every element, you just need an eye to see it!". You can connect to him personally on Instagram @bollyrahul

Padmini Peteri

Padmini Peteri is an avid reader who has a passion for writing her heart out. She writes short stories and poetry in both Hindi and English languages. To her, writing is healing and a way of expression. She mostly writes about mental health and social issues. She gets lost in the world of books,

of imagination, of poetries and stories. She believes in smiling and spreading happiness makes the world a better place to live in. Her writing finds wings on her Instagram handle @minithoughts_pp.

Saloni Wagle

Being a talkative soul, words have always meant a lot to Saloni. But it wasn't until she put them down on paper, that she realised they weren't just her necessity, but her passion. She was immediately intoxicated by the feeling of gratification of completing a piece, and thus began her journey as a writer. Though she enjoys writing prose as well, her poems what she is most proud of.

Prerna Agrawal

She is a girl for whom simplicity is the key to happiness. It wouldn't be always easy to do something, but she always tries to do what's right. She likes her coffee as she likes herself: sweet and strong. She wants to be a psychologist to be able to save people who are in depression. She believes God has given us one life and we should not waste that on worrying about something or with those people for whom we don't mean anything, therefore we must live our life to the fullest and be such a person who can inspire people.

Shreya Khemani

A scribbler from the heart and a Data Scientist as a professional, she believes that words hold immense power to impact people, to bring happiness, and to bring everlasting changes. She is here to share her opinions loud and clear because in the end, it's for the things that matter in life, as it's the words that make us feel better. You can find her on Instagram @scribbling_sky

Uzlifat Zahoor

She's from South Kashmir. Her way to write about unique verses gets inspiration from her nature and love. Sober and rhymes is what she fancies. She's currently working on a fantasy novel of her own and she's also a brilliant calligrapher.

Namita Das

Namita Das is an IT professional with an experience of 13 Years working with MNCs, on a break to raise her little munchkin. An engineer who wandered into writing codes, but her heart was always set on writing creatively. She is a frequent blogger which centers around humour. Apart from blogging a kiddie book with a concept to combine fun and learning is also work in progress. A quick visit to her blog "Pen It Rather Key It" is kind of stress buster with snazzy humorous writing pieces and keep readers abreast with latest happening. Namita takes keen interest in human psychology and loves to explore new places. She is based in Uganda with her husband and a cute kiddo with a dream to write bestselling book one day.

Meenakshi Ramswamy

Meenakshi Ramaswamy is a commerce graduate. She is in the habit of capping her thoughts in a lovesome manner. Flawless Night is her fervid oeuvre of nature.

Mohammed Mudassir

Mohammed Mudassir is a writer in his twenties from North England. Impacting the masses with his auspicious poetry and literature, he looks to inspire communities positively, with his introspective content with all kinds of people throughout the world. He is a sagacious man with an excellent perspective who encourages scrutiny upon the world's mysteries so that all views can be uncovered, and the world can be viewed in a new light. You can connect with him on Instagram at @ceaseless_wisdoms.

Neha Prashar

Neha is a business developer, a blogger, a traveller, a military wife and an aspiring author. In her journey from writing market research reports to writing stories, blogs, and poems, she has created various pearls with her literary skills. She loves to read in solace with her thoughts. Her works are inspired by daily life, emotions, fiction, and travels.

She is a loving mother and loves music and painting.

Vaishnavi Singh

Vaishnavi is a law student. She loves her legal field as there are so many things related to one's daily life and every day you tranquil many new things. She believes that one should live "life to express and not to impress" and this is what makes her write. She writes what she feels, for her letters are the best gift to express emotions and feelings. She is an extrovert person, she loves to explore life, she refuses to be bogged down by the past rather learn from the mistakes and move on. She believes life is not a competitive platform, rather it is a very beautiful thing to live and feel around.

Shikha Sharda

Shikha Sharda, better known by her pen name Shikha.S, is a writer and her ideas come from looking at life of ordinary people and their situations with a different perspective. She further says that she prefers to write about real life topics, more than imaginations and fantasies because real life content allows for a deeper understanding of the wondrous world we inhabit. Born and brought up in Delhi, she now lives in Noida. After doing her post-graduation in M.A. Honours (English), she opted a career of content writer with an intent of writing her own novel someday.

Divya Bora

By profession, Divya is in the field of finance. Her work requires her to study legal terms and numbers and by passion for words she loves to write. Writing is her source of freedom. In this way she sends her thoughts which she has seen and learnt in her life to you all. Writing gives her a sense of passion to do right with the help of words.

The Wanderer Mind

She is a wanderer who lives her life on her terms and sees the world differently. A thinker, explorer and an emotional being. A curious mind she is and wants to feel every bit of life she could cross through. She carries an ocean of love and care. She wants to reach out to all hearts and souls with her writing and emotions.

Nirosha Tomy

As a political science graduate of Delhi University, living amidst the cultural diversity of the national capital, Nirosha Tomy uses her personal experiences and that of the people around her to create a perfect blend of fact and fiction to produce an authentic literary work. She hopes to inspire and influence others to think, through her carefully curated writings.

Deepesha J.

She's an ordinary woman with an exquisite mind, striving to make a difference with one ink stroke at a time. Her eyes may have the wanderer's lust, but Mumbai's essence lies in her heart's crust. Law is her passion, writing her honeyed salvation. At the bewildering age of 22, she has a broader perspective to bind. The lady has a message to sign: "Read & Vibe, Unlearn & Unwind"

Jagruthi Kommuri

Jagruthi an e-commerce graduate, currently working and an MBA student, who started writing to express her feelings and loves to write to ignite a little hope and faith in the reader. She's a simple girl who finds solace in words and writes to spread love & positivity in the world. She believes kindness goes a long way when communicated through heart.

Disha Shinde

Disha Shinde is a student of 10th standard. She aspires to become an entrepreneur and a famous writer one day. She writes poems and blogs as a hobby. She loves reading and spending time with family, friends, and nature. She writes to motivate and wishes to bring a change through her words. She also enjoys arts and crafts and is concerned about the environment.

Swetha Nair

Swetha Nair is a Chartered Accountant based in Mumbai. She inculcated the habit of writing her journal since childhood where she would pour her heart down without bothering about the literary words, rhymes, or anything for that matter. Later to just crumble up the sheets as she did not want anyone to ever read it. During the lockdown she revisited her hobby and began to post few of her write-ups on Mirakee and Instagram with the handle @crumbled sheets. She hopes that you connect with her words and enjoy them.

9 788819 493244